FUN TO MAKE AND DO

By HANNAH TOFTS and ANNIE OWEN

Editor Diane James
Photography Jon Barnes

TWO CAN ™

PRINCETON ■ LONDON

CONTENTS

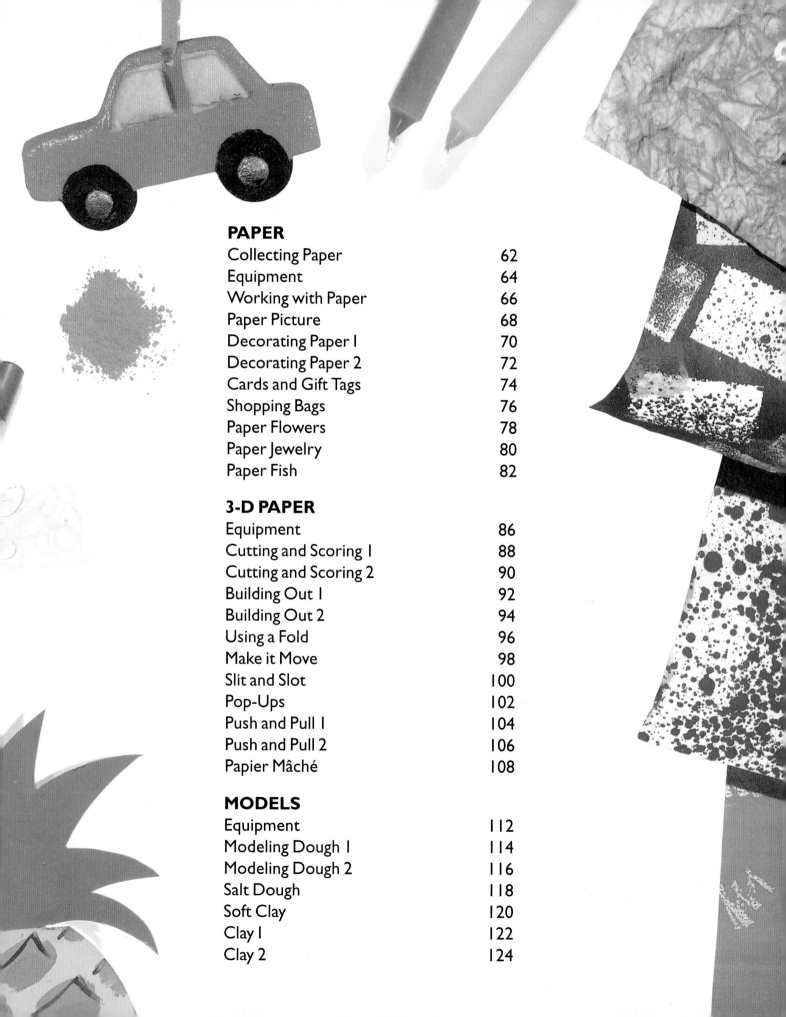

Published in the United States and Canada by
Two-Can Publishing LLC, 234 Nassau Street, Princeton, NJ 08542

© 2000 Two-Can Publishing
For information on Two-Can books and multimedia, call 1-609-921-6700, fax 1-609-921-3349,
or visit our Web site at http://www.two-canpublishing.com

'Two-Can' is a trademark of Two-Can Publishing.
Two-Can Publishing is a division of Zenith Entertainment plc, 43-45 Dorset Street, London W1H 4AB

ISBN 1-58728-111-2

1 2 3 4 5 6 7 8 9 10 02 01 00

Printed in Hong Kong by Wing King Tong

PAINT

CONTENTS

All of the things on these pages are used somewhere in the PAINT section of this book. You should be able to find most of them in your home or at school, but some you may have to buy from craft stores or toy stores.

Look out for things that might be useful – plastic spoons, plastic and aluminum foil containers, and scraps of fabric.

For most painting, you can use poster or tempera paints. But for some things you will need special paints.

It's useful to have a selection of fat and thin brushes – short, stiff brushes are good for stenciling and spattering.

Some painting can be extremely messy, so keep a good supply of newspaper to put on the floor.

colored candles

fabric paint pens

fabric paint

poster paint

poster paint

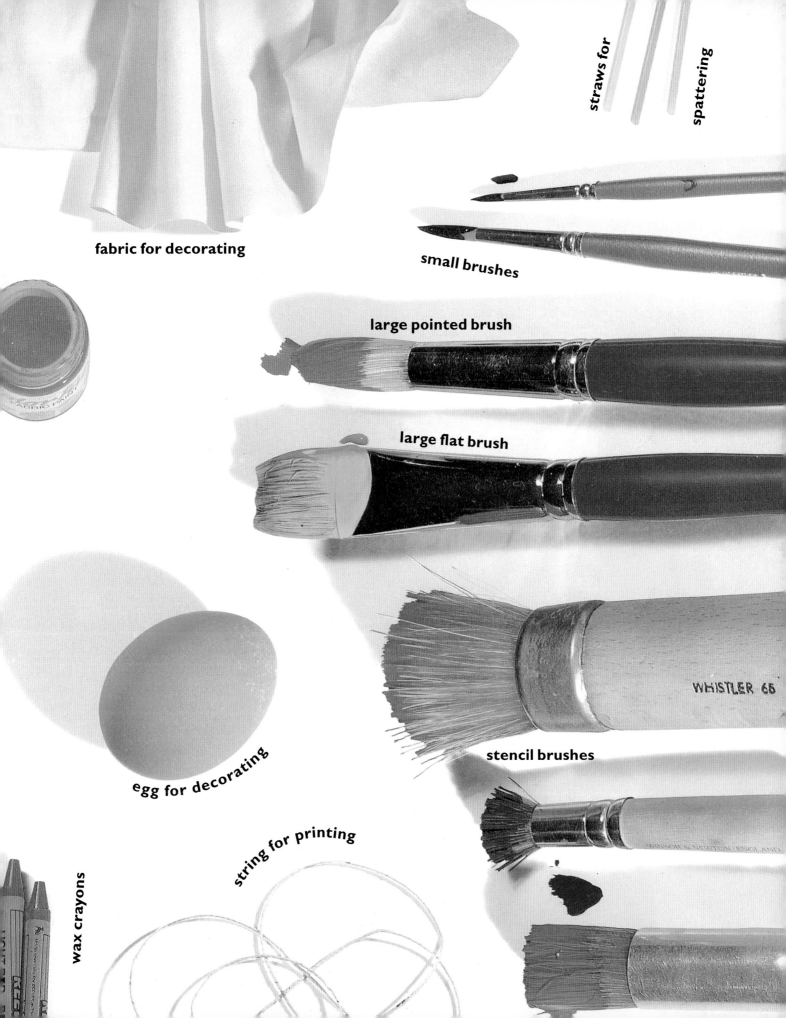

straws for spattering

fabric for decorating

small brushes

large pointed brush

large flat brush

WHISTLER 65

stencil brushes

egg for decorating

string for printing

wax crayons

Mixing your own colors can be very satisfying. Although you may sometimes get muddy colors, they will certainly be different!

Try adding more, or less, water when you are mixing paints to give different effects.

Color Mixing
Yellow + Red = Orange
Blue + Yellow = Green
Blue + Red = Purple

Look around the home for empty yogurt containers, plastic trays, and lids to mix paints in.

Keep your eyes open for useful brushes such as old toothbrushes, small scrubbing brushes, and paintbrushes.
If no one wants them, you can cut them down and use them for stenciling or spattering.

Try not to damage your brushes by being rough with them when you are mixing. Moving them in just one direction will keep the hairs smooth and make the brushes last longer.

Anyone can join in the fun of hand and feet painting. First, put down plenty of newspaper because it can be very messy!

Cover the soles of your feet with fairly thick paint and make footprints on a large sheet of paper. You should get an interesting effect, and the paint will wash off afterward.

After a bit of practice, try making patterns using both hands and feet. It is best if one person is in charge of the others.

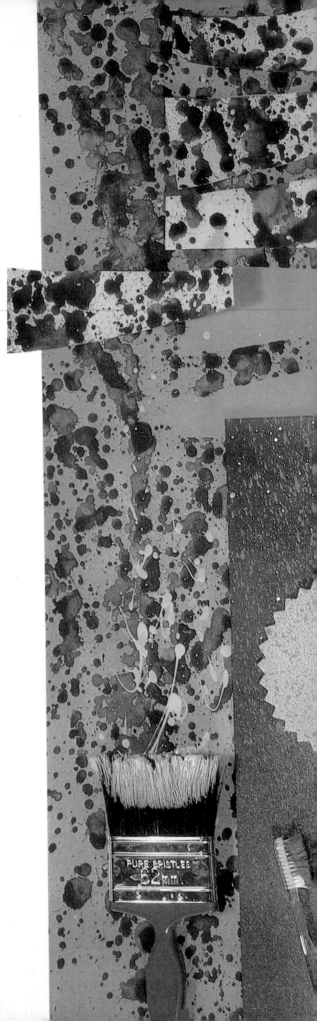

Straw Painting

Drip some runny paint onto a sheet of paper. Get close to the paint and blow gently through a straw. The paint should make strange patterns as it spreads across the paper.

If you add a second color right away, the colors will mix and blend together in places. If you don't want this effect, wait until the first color is dry.

Spatter with Small Brushes

Find a selection of small brushes with short, stiff bristles, such as old toothbrushes or nailbrushes. Dip one of the brushes in medium-thick paint. Hold the brush over a large sheet of paper and run a small piece of cardboard down the bristles. You should get a fine speckled effect on the paper.

Try masking out areas by laying cardboard shapes on clean paper. Spatter paint over the shapes. When you lift off the shapes, there will be matching shapes left behind.

Spatter with Large Brushes

Find the kind of paintbrush normally used to paint walls. Cover it with medium-thick paint. Stand over a large sheet of paper and flick the brush up and down. You should get an interesting effect of large speckles. Try using different colors on top of each other.

All of these methods are very messy, so make sure all surfaces are well covered.

▼ Fold a large sheet of paper in half. Unfold the paper and drop some fairly runny paint along the fold and on either side of it. Fold the paper along the original fold again, and smooth it over with your hand. You can use one color or several colors. If you don't want the colors to run together, allow each color to dry before you drop on blobs of the next color.

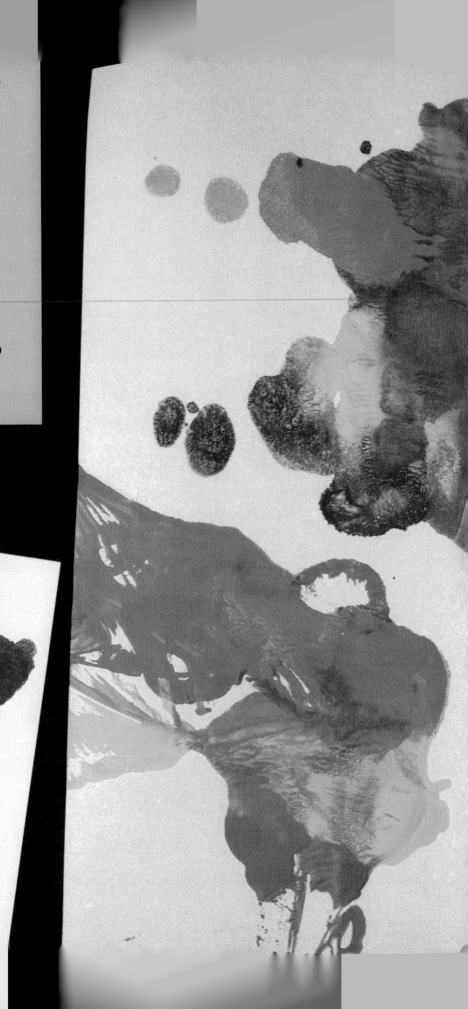

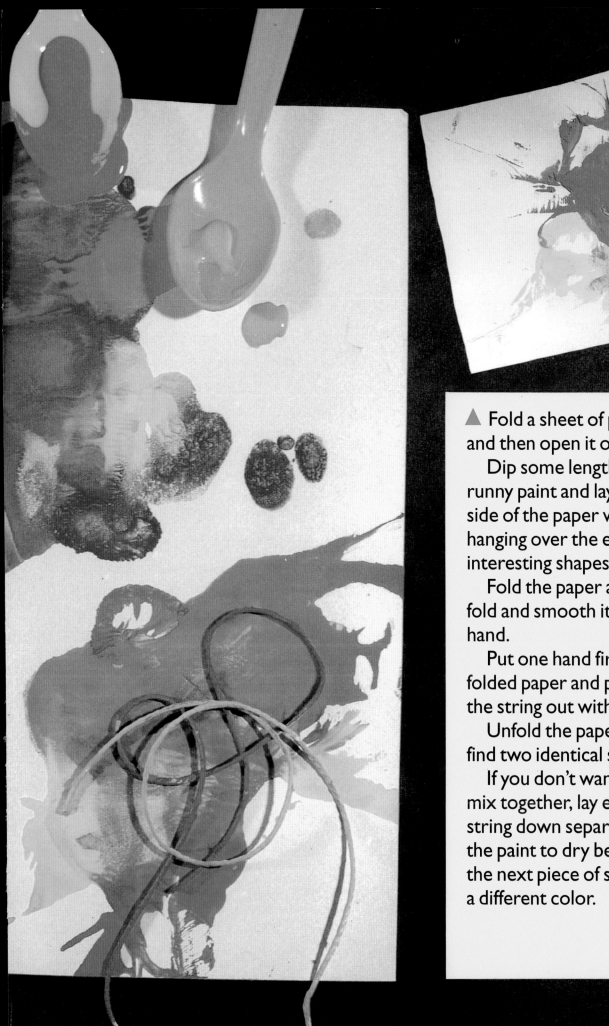

▲ Fold a sheet of paper in half and then open it out flat again.

Dip some lengths of string in runny paint and lay them on one side of the paper with the ends hanging over the edge. Try to make interesting shapes with the string.

Fold the paper along the original fold and smooth it over with your hand.

Put one hand firmly on top of the folded paper and pull the ends of the string out with your other hand.

Unfold the paper and you will find two identical swirly patterns.

If you don't want the colors to mix together, lay each piece of string down separately and allow the paint to dry before using the next piece of string with a different color.

► Wax and paint do not mix, but you can get some interesting effects by using them together. Make simple patterns on a sheet of paper with a wax crayon. Paint over the pattern with runny paint. The paint will not stay where the wax marks are.

▼ Look for something that has an interesting texture – the bark of a tree, a piece of rough wood, or some bumpy glass. Tape a piece of paper over the textured surface and rub carefully with a wax crayon.

Paint over the wax pattern with runny paint.

► Draw a picture or make a pattern with colored wax crayons. Using a thick brush and fairly runny paint, cover the whole picture. The wax crayons will show through leaving a painted background to your picture.

▼ Color a sheet of paper with different colored wax crayons – there shouldn't be any white paper showing. Paint over the wax with thick black paint – you may need several layers – and leave to dry.

Scrape some of the paint away with the back of a spoon or the end of a pencil. The wax crayon will show through where you scrape the paint away.

Try making patterns with vegetables and paint! Look for vegetables with interesting textures.

Start with a carrot. You can slice the carrot across the middle or lengthwise. Dip the cut surface in some thick paint and press onto a sheet of paper.

Cut a potato in half. You can either scoop out a pattern in the cut surface or, using a knife, cut away a section to leave a raised pattern. Dip the potato halves in thick paint and print onto paper. A cabbage cut in quarters also makes a good print.

Try experimenting with other vegetables cut in different ways.

Paste Recipe

1 cup flour   3 cups water

1. In a pan, mix a little of the water with the flour to make a smooth paste.

2. Add the rest of the water and ask a grown-up to heat the mixture until it boils – stirring all the time. When it is boiling, turn the heat down and let the mixture simmer until the paste thickens.

When the paste is cold, spoon a little into some small containers. Add some paint to each container and mix well.

Cut out some pieces of cardboard to use as scrapers. Try cutting notches in the end of one piece to make an interesting shape.

Cover a piece of paper with paste paint using a thick brush.

Using cardboard scrapers, scrape away areas of the paste paint. Try making different marks by using different sizes of scrapers.

By now, you should have lots of patterns and pictures that need framing! Or you might want to make frames for your postcards and photographs.

First cut some frames from pieces of cardboard. Make sure that the inside of the frame is slightly smaller than the picture you want to frame.

To get a layered effect, start with a small frame. Glue a slightly larger frame on top of it, and then glue a larger one still on top of that.

Try using methods such as spattering, wax and paint, and paste paint to decorate your frames.

If you want to use paste paint, glue the painted paper onto the cardboard before you cut out the frame.

You can buy special stencil paper from craft stores, but ordinary cardboard works as well.

You will also need a craft knife, a stencil brush with short, stiff hairs, and some thick paint.

Draw simple shapes onto your piece of cardboard.

Cut out the shapes with a craft knife, but ask for help if you haven't used one before.

You can stencil onto most surfaces — paper, cardboard, fabric, and wood. But it is best to try your idea out on paper first.

Hold down the stencil firmly with one hand and dab the paint on — inside the stencil — with a stencil brush.

You can use different colors, but allow each color to dry before using the next.

Not all Easter eggs are made of chocolate! These eggs have been hard-boiled and decorated with wax crayons, candle wax, food coloring, and onion skins.

Always ask for help when boiling the eggs and make sure they are cold before you decorate them.

Treat the eggs gently when you are decorating them, or they will crack!

Onion Skin Eggs

Wrap an egg in layers of onion skin. Put the egg and onion skins on a piece of fabric, or push them into the toe of an old stocking, and tie up the bundle. Hard-boil the egg. When the water has cooled, take the egg out and unwrap it. It will be beautifully marbled in an orange-brown color.

Wax and Dye Eggs 1

Draw a pattern on an egg (before hard-boiling) with a white wax crayon or a piece of candle. Don't press too hard!

Put a few drops of food coloring into some water in a pan. Ask a grown-up to hard-boil the egg in it. When the egg has cooked, take it out and leave it to cool. The food coloring colors the egg in the places where there is no wax.

Wax and Dye Eggs 2

For this method, you must ask a grown-up to help with dripping the wax onto the egg and using the oven. Light a candle and let blobs of wax drop onto the egg. Put some food coloring and water into a saucer and gently roll the egg around. Drop some more candle wax onto the egg and roll it around in a saucer of darker food coloring and water.

Put the egg on a baking dish in a medium-hot oven. After a few minutes, take the egg out and wipe off any excess wax. These eggs are for decoration only!

The plates, knives, forks, and spoons on the tablecloth may look real, but you can't pick them up because they have been painted on.

If you use special fabric paints and pens, you can wash the fabric over and over and the paint won't come out!

It helps to put a piece of cardboard under the area you are painting to keep the fabric steady.

Fabric pens are good for doing outlines and detailed work, but use paints and a fat brush for larger areas.

Most fabric paints should be left to dry and then ironed, but always read the instructions carefully and ask a grown-up for help using the iron.

Marbling is not difficult to do and you can use marbled papers for writing on, for wrapping gifts, or covering books. Every sheet will look different!

Find a baking dish at least one inch (2.5 cm) deep and large enough to hold the size of paper you want to marble.

Fill the dish almost to the top with water and add a few drops of vinegar.

Drop small blobs of any oil-based paint onto the surface of the water and swirl them around with a stick, pencil, or cardboard comb.

Hold opposite ends of a clean sheet of paper and lay it on the surface of the water. Try to make sure there are no air bubbles. Gently lift the paper off and put it – colored side up – on some newspaper to dry.

Some of the different effects you can get are shown over the page. Try making more than one print from the same paints.

PRINT

CONTENTS

Here are some of the things you will need to start printing. Almost anything with a raised surface will give a print, so look for different textures.

You can use almost any paint for printing, but oil paint gives you the best results. If you use oil paint, you will need a good supply of rags and turpentine for cleaning up.

Look for flat surfaces to roll you paint onto for printing – linoleum or the shiny side of a piece of hardboard are best.

Be very careful when using a craft knife – ask for help if you have problems with cutting! Always use a piece of thick cardboard or linoleum to cut on.

block of wood

Scotch™ tape

craft knife

cardboard and paper

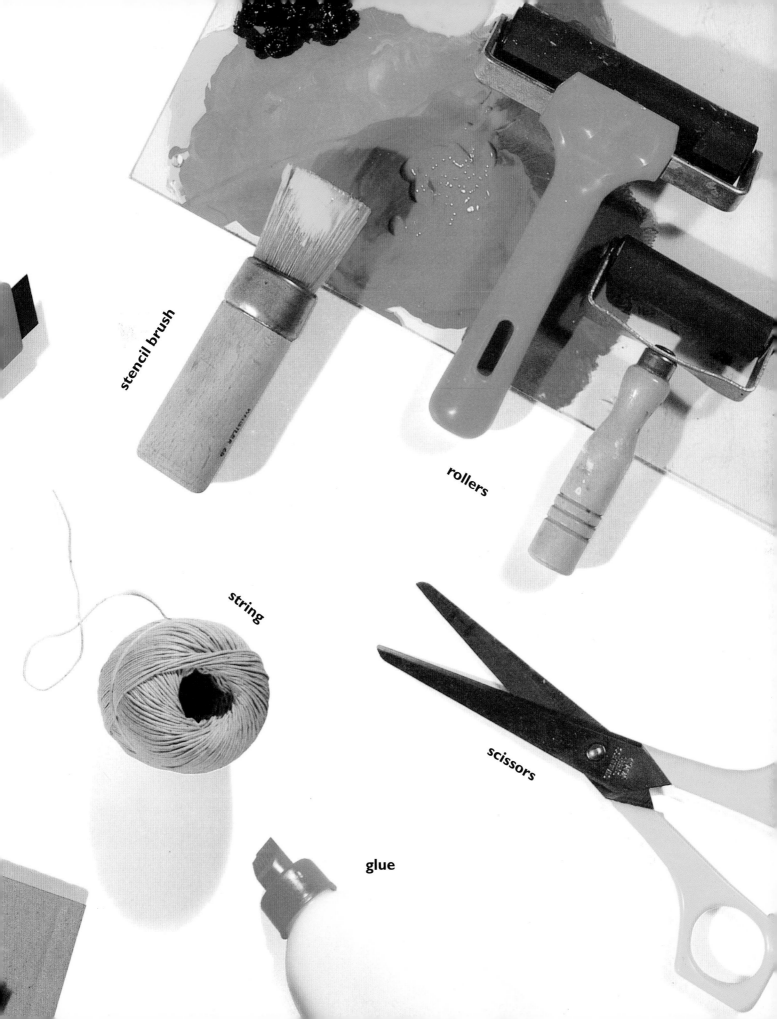

stencil brush

rollers

string

scissors

glue

You can take a print from most things that have a textured surface – rough, knobbly, or patterned. Look both indoors and outdoors for things with different textures.

You will have to cover the object that you want to take a print from with paint. Make sure you will not be doing any permanent damage. If in doubt, use paint that will wash off easily.

Use thick paint and a large brush or roller to cover the surface you want to print from. Lay a sheet of paper over the object and press down firmly and smoothly, or run a clean roller over the paper. Lift the paper off gently and leave your print to dry. Try experimenting by combining different textures.

The prints above were made from a rough plank of wood, a car tire, and a manhole cover. The ones on the left were made with blocks of wood and leaves.

Here are some suggestions for making simple printing blocks that you can use over and over again.

Using an old rolling pin, wrap string around and around it and glue the ends firmly. Mix some fairly thick paint on a piece of linoleum or hardboard (shiny side). Roll the rolling pin up and down the paint to coat the string. Make a print by rolling the rolling pin smoothly along a piece of paper.

You can make other printing blocks by gluing string arranged in a pattern onto a block of wood. Or you can wind thick cord around a block of wood, or glue on lengths of broken pasta. Try taking more than one print before covering the block with paint again.

Think of ways you could use
your printed papers — as wrapping
paper, for covering books, or even
as wallpaper!

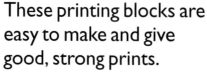

These printing blocks are easy to make and give good, strong prints.

Use pieces of thick cardboard for the printing blocks. From another piece of cardboard, cut straight strips. Glue the strips onto the printing block to make a pattern.

Cover the printing block with fairly thick paint using a roller. Press the block firmly on to a sheet of paper and smooth over it with a clean roller.

Try using strips of torn paper or thin cardboard instead of straight strips. Make two or three blocks in the same way, but use paint of different colors to print each one. See how many different patterns you can make by alternating the colors.

These printing blocks are made by cutting shapes out of pieces of cardboard. Cut two rectangles from an old cardboard box using a craft knife. Ask a grown-up to help.

Cut out shapes – diamonds, triangles, squares, and rectangles – from one of the pieces of cardboard, to make a kind of stencil. Cover this with fairly thick paint and make a print. Now cut shapes out of the other piece of cardboard. You will be printing this stencil on top of the first print, so try to use shapes that will work well together. Use a different color to print the second block on top of the first.

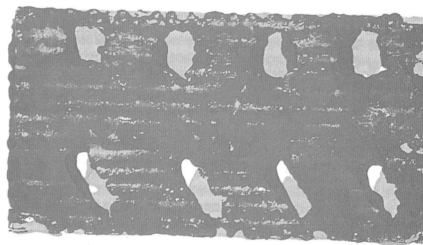

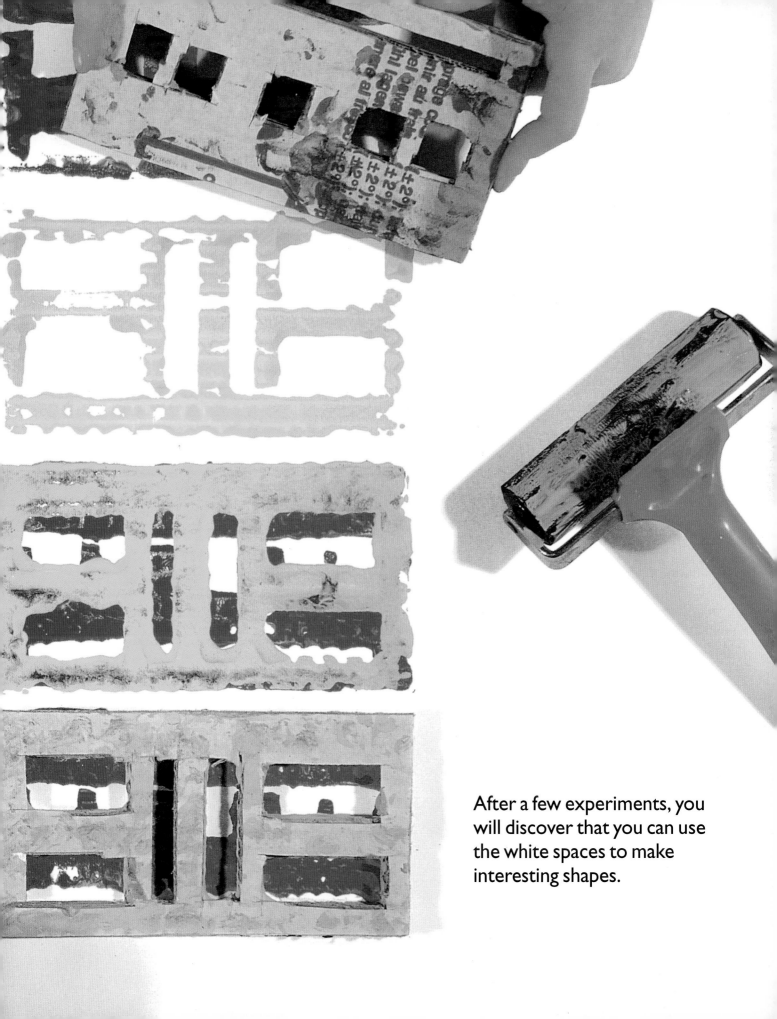

After a few experiments, you will discover that you can use the white spaces to make interesting shapes.

Here is a way to make several prints of the same picture. First, make a color drawing and then trace it.

For each color that you want to use, cut a separate piece of cardboard – each one the same size as your tracing. These will be your printing blocks. Lay your tracing on each of these blocks in turn and trace all the shapes that are the same color. So you should have a different printing block for each color.

Next, trace over your tracing onto another piece of cardboard and then cut out all the individual shapes. Glue each shape into position on the printing block for its color.

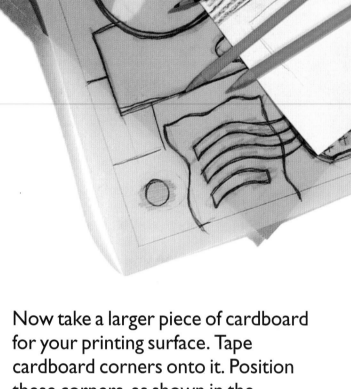

Now take a larger piece of cardboard for your printing surface. Tape cardboard corners onto it. Position these corners, as shown in the picture, so that they will hold the blocks firmly while you are printing.

Now you are ready to print! Lay a sheet of paper – the same size as the blocks – in the corners. Roll paint over one of the blocks. Using the corners as guides, carefully place the block over the paper. Press down on the block and then lift it off. Repeat the process with the other blocks, remembering to change the color each time!

Try building up a picture using printed shapes. Cut shapes from stiff cardboard using a craft knife. Ask a grown-up to help. Use a strip of cardboard as a handle. Fold it in half and bend back the two ends. Stick the ends firmly to the back of your cardboard shapes. Cut up old cardboard tubes and use the edges to print curves. Use thick paint and watery paint to get different effects. Try overprinting shapes while they are still wet.

To make a stencil, see page 26. Place the stencil on a sheet of paper and use a stencil brush – with short, stiff hairs – to stipple the paint on.

You can use the shape cut from the stencil to make a print. Lay the shape on a piece of paper and spatter paint over it (see page 14). Use a nailbrush or an old toothbrush and a piece of cardboard to spatter with. Always spatter away from you!

Try making this pattern by laying cardboard rectangles on a piece of black paper and stippling over them with white paint. Reposition the rectangles and stipple over with yellow paint.

Try experimenting with different shapes to build up your own patterns.

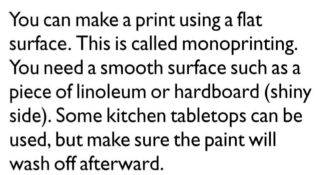

You can make a print using a flat surface. This is called monoprinting. You need a smooth surface such as a piece of linoleum or hardboard (shiny side). Some kitchen tabletops can be used, but make sure the paint will wash off afterward.

To make a pattern like the one above, cover the flat surface with fairly thick paint. Use a piece of cardboard to scrape away patterns from the paint. Lay a sheet of paper carefully over the pattern. Gently smooth the paper down with your hand. Peel the paper back to reveal your print. Try making more than one print.

Another method of monoprinting is to paint a simple picture straight onto your flat surface. Lay a sheet of paper over the picture and carefully smooth it down. Lift off the paper and leave the print to dry.

Try printing a picture for your bedroom wall! You can use all sorts of different printing methods in the same picture, but keep the shapes as simple as possible. Start with the background and build up the picture bit by bit.

Patterns make good pictures too. Look at the leaf pattern here and try to work out your own patterns using different printing blocks and stencils.

Here are some examples of printed papers using methods described in this section. Try making a selection of your own designs. You can use printed paper to cover books, to write on, to wrap presents, and as pictures for your bedroom wall!

Try making your own writing paper. You can print border designs using simple shapes, and you can personalize the paper by printing your name on it! If you want to print your name or initials, try using very simple shapes to make the letters. Turn the page and you will find some suggestions for printing your own envelopes.

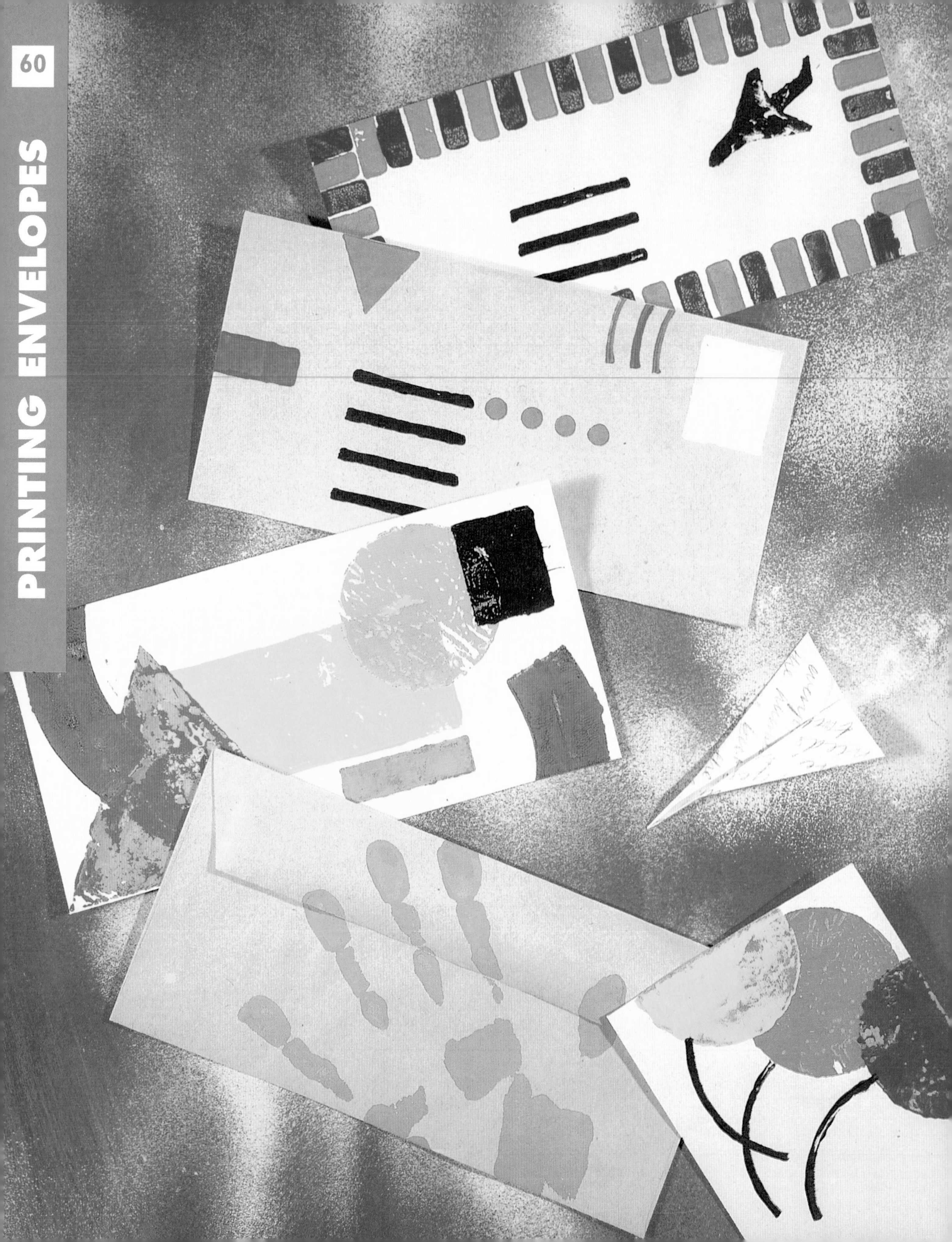

PAPER

CONTENTS

Offres Meublés 4e
MARAIS 5.500 F
MARAIS GD LUXE
RESIDENCE
PORTE DE VINCENNES
USAirmail
BY AIR MAIL
PAR AVION
MIT LUFTPOST

You don't have to buy expensive paper to make any of the things in this section of the book. Look at all the different papers on these pages. Now look around your home to see what you can find – old wrapping paper, brown paper, the insides of envelopes, corrugated cardboard used for packing, used stamps, postcards, cereal boxes, candy wrappers, and old newspapers.

Start making a collection of different papers now! Later on, you will find many different ways to decorate plain paper.

When you have gathered together a collection of different papers, you are almost ready to start! All of the things on these pages are used somewhere in the PAPER section of this book for cutting, gluing, decorating, and assembling. You will probably be able to find most of them in your home, but you may have to buy some of them from craft or toy stores.

Be very careful when using scissors and craft knives – ask for help if you have any problems with cutting! Always use a piece of thick cardboard or linoleum when you are cutting with a sharp knife.

straws for spattering and decorating

ruler for straight lines

scissors

paint and brushes for decorating paper

toothpicks for flower stems

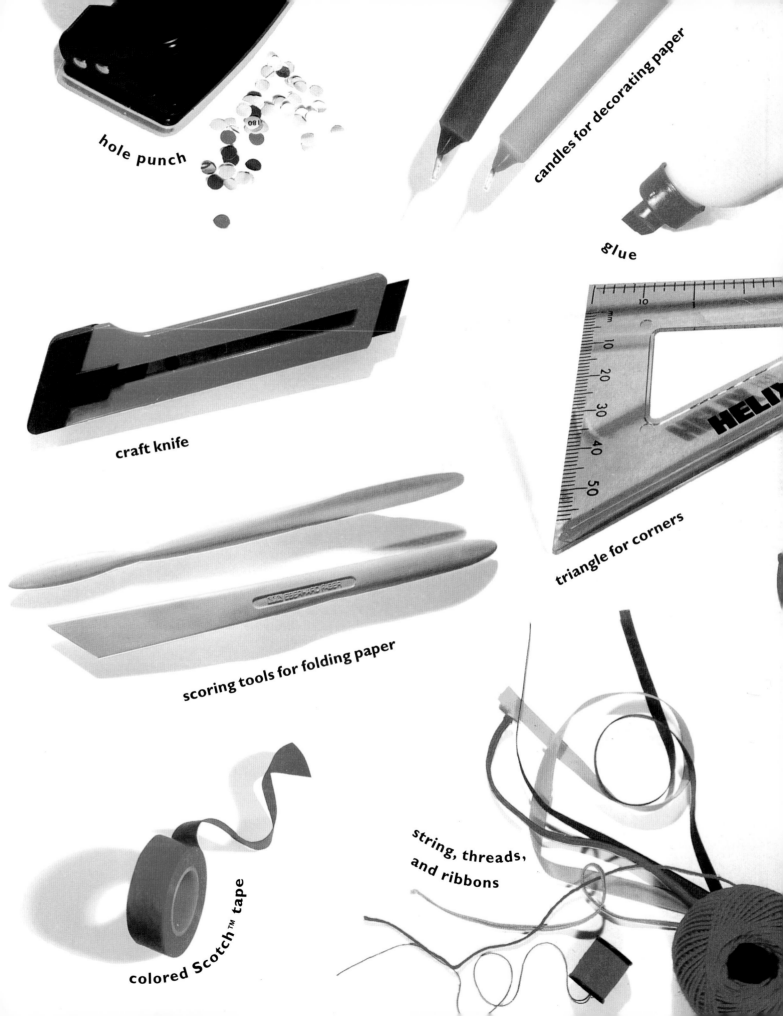

hole punch

candles for decorating paper

glue

craft knife

triangle for corners

scoring tools for folding paper

colored Scotch™ tape

string, threads, and ribbons

Paper Curls

Cut a long, thin strip of colored paper. Wrap the strip tightly around a pencil or knitting needle. Pull the pencil or needle out and you will have a paper curl.

Paper Beads

Glue two sheets of colored paper together. Tear out triangles and roll them up tightly, starting at the wide end.

Crumpled Paper

Give paper an interesting texture by crumpling it up. When you are collecting papers, look for paper that has already been crumpled up.

Weaving Paper

Cut out some long, thin strips of different colored paper. Weave the strips in and out, as in the picture. If you want the strips to stay in position, glue them onto a backing sheet.

Glue and Tear

You can make paper stronger by gluing two layers together. If you glue two different colors together and then tear out shapes, you will get an interesting edge. If you glue three or more layers of paper together, you will get an even stronger paper – more like thin cardboard.

Accordion Folds

Take a long, thin strip of paper and practice making accordion folds, or pleats. They can be as large or as small as you like. Later on, you will see how to use pleated paper to make jewelry and paper flowers.

Cutting, Punching, and Tearing

Cutting paper gives a smooth edge, while tearing leaves a ragged edge. Both methods give interesting effects and are used in this section. Use a hole punch to punch small, round holes. Keep the pieces – they may be useful!

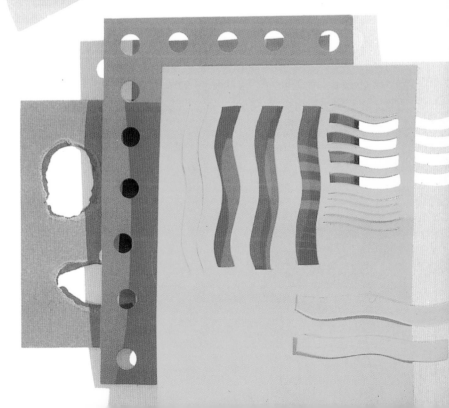

If you look carefully at this picture, you will see that it is made almost entirely from different kinds of paper.

The papers here include newspaper, insides of envelopes, brown paper, wrapping paper, wax paper, and tissue paper, as well as plastic straws, and aluminum foil. Look around your home to see how many different kinds of paper you can find.

Draw a rough sketch of your idea and decide which papers will be best.

Cut and tear the papers into shapes and glue them in position, starting with the background.

Remember that you can bend, curl, and crumple paper and thin cardboard to make interesting shapes. Look at pages 66 and 67 to find out how to weave paper and make accordion folds.

Here are some examples of different methods for decorating paper. Turn over the page to see the results.

Sponge Printing
Try dipping differently shaped sponges – large and small – into fairly thick paint. Press the sponges onto the paper.

Object Printing
Look for objects that have an interesting shape or a raised texture. Dip them into fairly thick paint and press onto the paper.

Wax and Paint
Make a pattern on the paper with wax crayons or candles. Paint over the wax marks with medium-thick paint. The paint will not stay where the wax marks are.

Crumpled Paper
Crumple up a small piece of paper and dip it into thick paint. Press it onto the paper to make a print.

Spattering
This is a very quick and easy method for decorating paper. Dip a large paintbrush into thick paint and either flick or shake it over the paper.

Here are some papers that have been decorated using the methods described on the previous page.

Experiment with the suggestions in this section and try out your own ideas too.

❶ ❻ Spatter painting

❷ ❾ Crumpled-paper printing

❸ Crumpled paper

❹ Sponge printing

❺ ❽ Paste paper (see page 22)

❼ Wax and paint

❿ Sponge and object printing

You don't need paints or colored pencils to make these cards and gift tags! All you need is colored paper, glue, scissors, and a craft knife. As a grown-up to help.

Slit and Slot Card

Fold a sheet of colored paper in half. Make slits from the top to the bottom, using a craft knife. Leave a border of at least one inch (2.5 cm) around the card. Weave different colored strips of paper in and out of the slits.

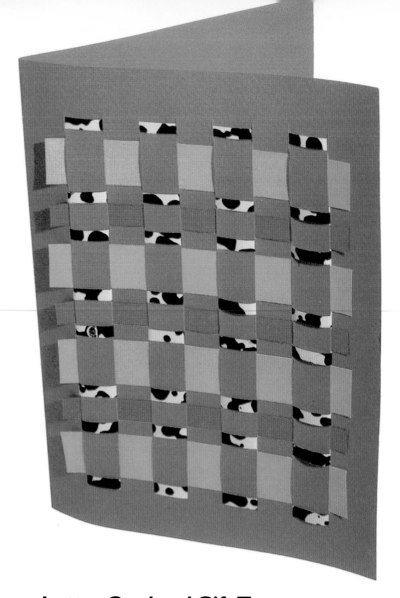

Letter Card and Gift Tag

Paste together two sheets of paper of different colors and fold in half. Using a craft knife, cut out the shape of a letter from the front of the card. Keep the letter that you cut out and punch a hole in it. Thread a piece of cord through the hole to make a gift tag.

Punch and Tear Card

Paste together two sheets of paper of different colors and fold in half to make a card. Pierce holes in the front of the card with a pencil and tear back strips of paper to make a pattern.

Cut Paper Card

Fold a sheet of colored paper in half. Using a craft knife, cut wavy slits and wavy shapes in the front of the card. Glue the shapes you cut out on the front of the card.

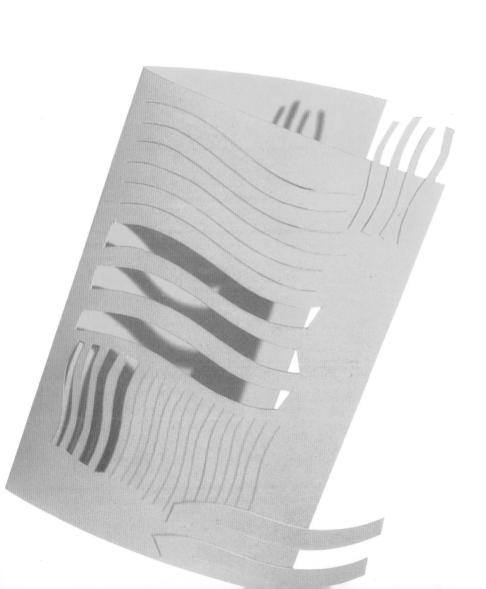

Gift Tags

Cut triangles or other shapes from colored paper. Punch holes in the tops of these shapes and thread a ribbon through. Write a message on the tag and attach it to a gift.

First decide how big you want your shopping bag to be.

1. On the back of a sheet of decorated paper, draw out a plan like the one at the top of the page. The pieces marked "A" will be the sides of the bag and they should each be the same width. The pieces marked "B" will be the front and back of the bag. These should also equal each other, but be wider than "A". The pieces marked "C" will be the bottom of the bag. They should be slightly narrower than "A".

2. Cut out corners, as shown in picture 2. Use a scoring tool to score all the dotted lines marked. The height of the triangles – marked "X" – should equal half the width of the sides of the bag (also marked "X").

3. Fold over and glue the top of the bag. This makes a strong, neat edge.

4. You can either use a hole punch to punch holes for cord at the top of the bag (front and back), or you can make small slits to thread ribbon through.

1.

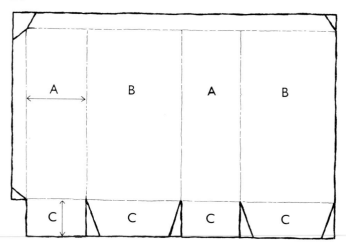

2.

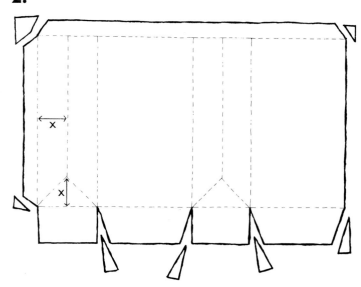

3.

4.

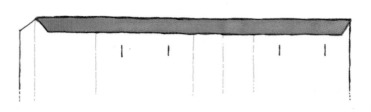

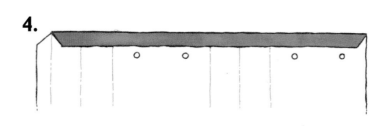

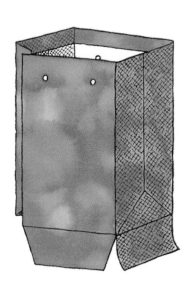

8. Slot cord or ribbon through the holes for handles.

5. Glue the bag together at the flap edge.

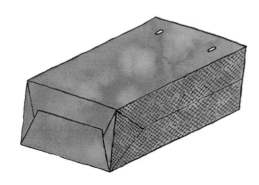

6. Fold the bottom flaps under and glue.

7. Gently push in the sides along the scored lines.

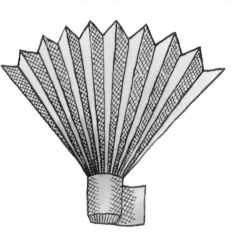

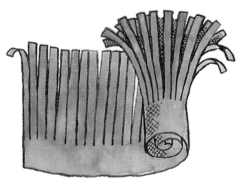

PAPER FLOWERS

Here are some suggestions for making paper flowers, but try your own ideas too!

Pleat a strip of colored paper. Pinch one end together and glue a strip of paper around to hold it.

Cut a long strip of colored paper. Make cuts along the length as shown above. Roll up the paper and bend the petals back. Try using different colored papers. Add leaves and a stem.

To make stems for your paper flowers, wrap a thin strip of green paper around a toothpick. Glue or tape the ends. You could also use a straw cut into short lengths and painted green.

Cut out different shapes for leaves as shown above. Score down the center of each leaf and fold. Leaves are good for covering up joins between flowers and stems.

The flower shown above was made by cutting separate petals, overlapping them and gluing them together. The paper curls were made by wrapping thin strips of paper around a pencil.

Cut petal shapes in a long strip of paper, as shown above. Roll the flower up and fold back the petals. Tissue paper makes good roses. Try making different shapes of petal.

Woven Earrings

Cut some thin strips of paper of different colors. Weave the strips in and out. When you have made a woven square, cut out a piece of paper the same size and glue it to the back of the woven square. Glue an earring attachment to the back.

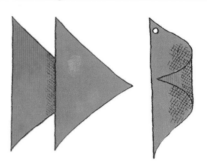

Triangle Earrings

Glue together two paper triangles of different colors. Curl the triangle around the handle of a wooden spoon. Pierce the top of each triangle and thread an earring attachment through them.

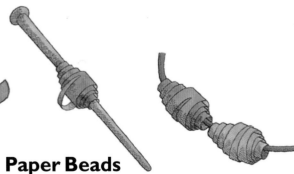

Paper Beads

Cut out a long, thin paper triangle. Starting at the wide end, roll the triangle around a knitting needle. Pull the needle out. Make a collection of beads and string them onto colored cord.

Pleated Brooch

Cut out two paper triangles. Pleat the triangles, as shown in the picture. Glue the long edges together. Pinch the pleats together in the middle. Wrap a thin strip of paper around the middle and glue it to hold the pleats in place. Glue a brooch attachment to the back.

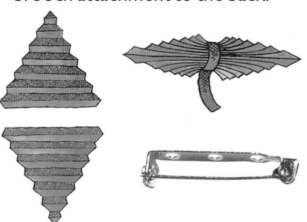

Accordion Bracelet

Take two long strips of paper. Glue the ends together at right angles. Keep folding one strip over the other, as shown in the picture. Glue the ends together. Accordion folds stretch and you should be able to slip the bracelet over your wrist easily.

You should be able to find earring attachments in craft stores. You may also find barrettes, to which you can glue paper bows or flowers.

These fish don't need feeding and you can make them any color you like! If you can't find a goldfish bowl, an old fish tank or a large glass jar will work just as well. Turn the page for the instructions.

Cut some simple fish shapes out of colored paper or thin cardboard. Using a craft knife, cut patterns in the fish or use a pencil to punch holes. Try gluing different colored cardboard behind the cutout shapes.

Next make a lid for your aquarium. Turn your chosen container upside down onto a piece of cardboard and draw around it. Cut out the shape. Use Scotch™ tape to attach different lengths of thread to the fish and to the cardboard lid. Put the lid on the bowl and watch your fish swimming around!

You can make watery shapes by using the insides of envelopes, and strips of curled paper make good seaweed.

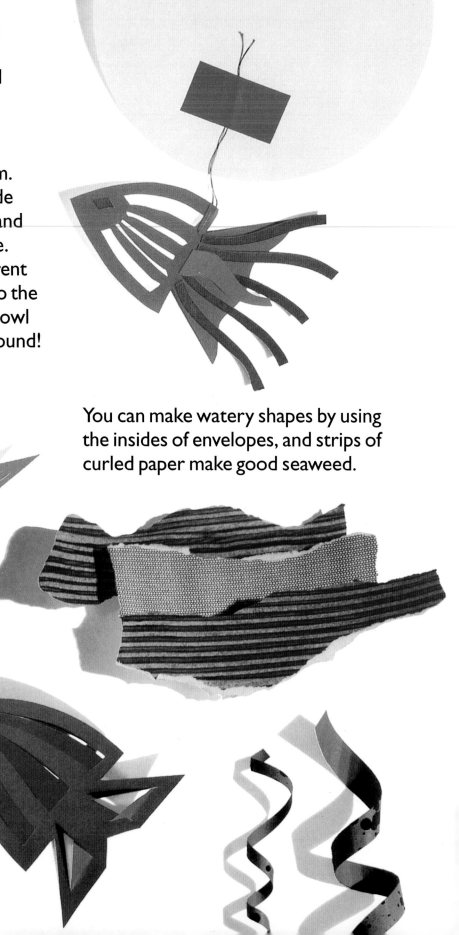

3-D PAPER

CONTENTS

In this section, you will find lots of different ways to make 3-D (three dimensional) shapes out of flat paper and cardboard. Make a collection of empty packages and boxes, cardboard tubes, and old egg boxes. Look for cardboard that has an interesting texture, such as corrugated cardboard. Be very careful when using a craft knife. Ask for help from a grown-up and always use a piece of thick cardboard or linoleum to cut on.

cardboard packages and boxes

craft knife

cardboard tubes

cardboard and paper

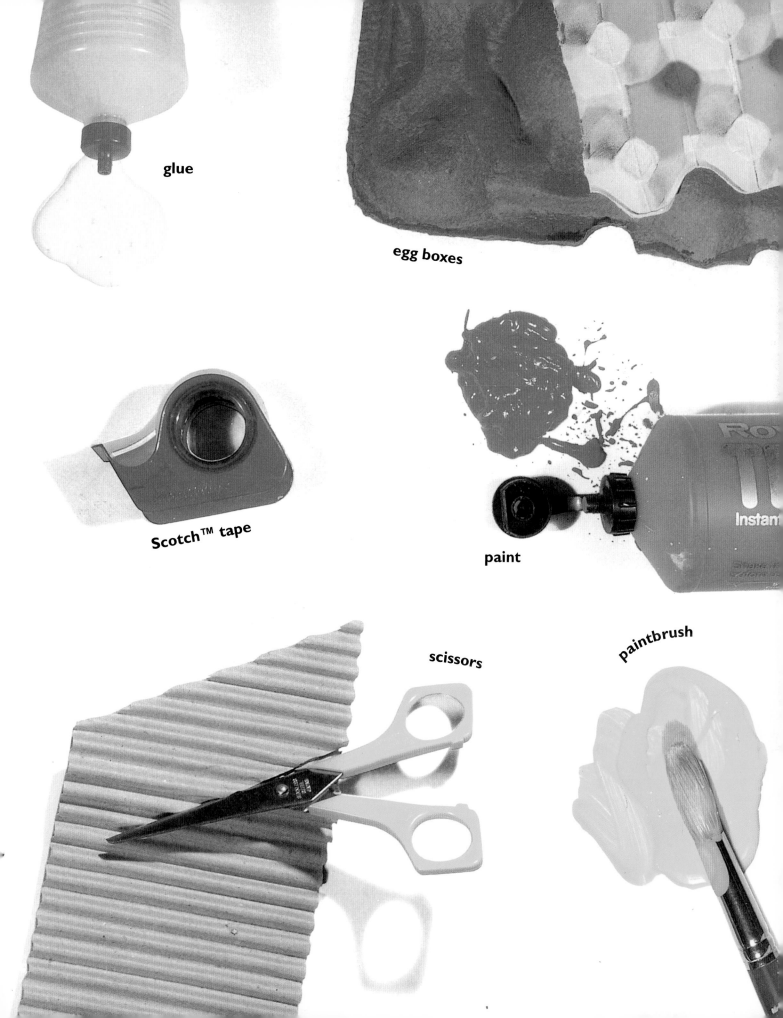

glue

egg boxes

Scotch™ tape

paint

scissors

paintbrush

Here are some suggestions for altering the shape of a flat piece of paper using simple cuts. Try cutting half-squares, circles, and triangles such as the ones at the top of the picture. Fold back every other strip of paper.

To make wavy triangles similar to those in the picture below, first score the wavy shapes on the paper. Cut triangles from one score line to the other. Fold the triangles upward. Try scoring and cutting other simple shapes.

Try cutting wide strips out of the paper and rolling the ends around a fat pencil, to make paper rolls.

Be very careful when cutting with a craft knife!

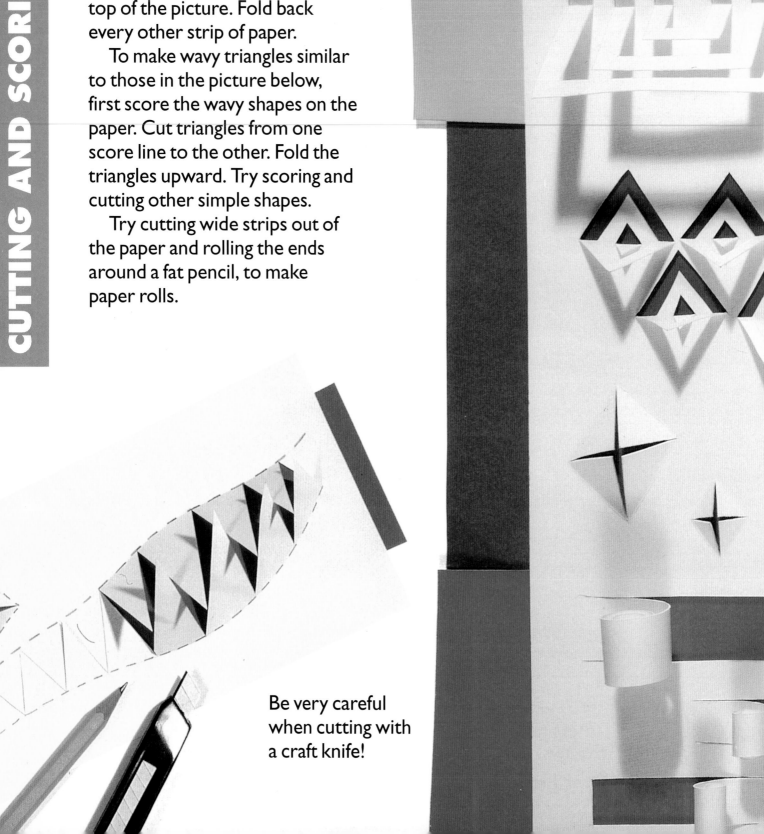

Here are some more ideas for cutting and scoring using accordion folds (see page 67). Score straight lines down a sheet of paper or thin cardboard using a ruler and a scoring tool. Make accordion folds along the score lines.

Use a pencil and ruler to draw squares or triangles in the center of a fold. The picture below shows you how to do this. Score along the dotted lines, and cut along the solid lines with a craft knife. Gently push the shapes up or down and away from the fold.

This picture was made simply by gluing cardboard shapes on top of each other. First, sketch out a rough design and work out how your layers will build up. Cut shapes from thick, soft cardboard and paint them. Glue the shapes in position. Watch how the shapes begin to make shadows as they build up.

To make a 3-D picture such as this one, you will need a good collection of interesting shapes. Look for lots of different boxes, tubes, cartons, and packaging materials. Lay out your collection and play around with the shapes until you have a well-balanced pattern. Either paint the shapes before you glue them down or use spray paint afterward.

Make your shapes stand up! Fold a sheet of cardboard or stiff paper in half. Draw a shape on the cardboard and cut around it. Do not cut along the fold, or your shape will not stand up!

To make the dog shown here, you will also need a head. This is cut out separately. Leave a tab on the end to slot into a slit made in the body. The pineapple leaves are made in the same way.

When slotting shapes together, make sure that the slit is exactly the same length as the tab you will slot into it. Glue or tape the tab in position on the inside.

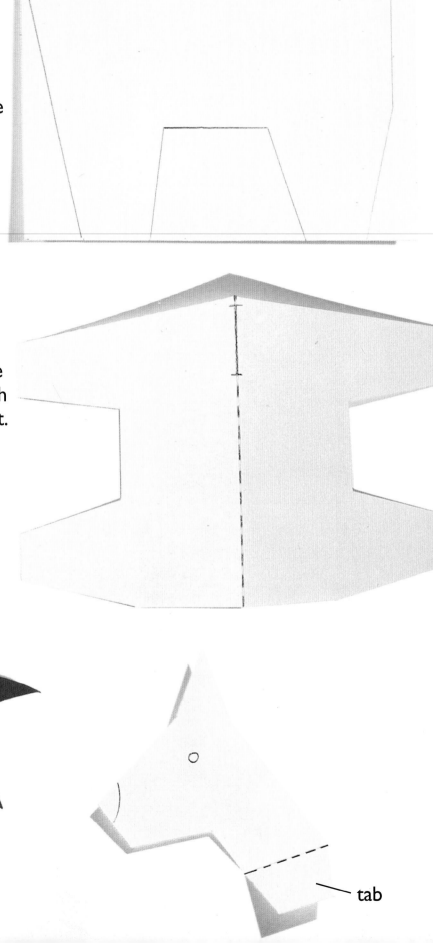

tab

By using "split pins," which you can buy in stationery and craft stores, you can make models that move! Try to find cardboard that is fairly thick but soft, such as old fruit boxes.

First, decide on the shape of your model and which pieces you want to move.

On the crocodile, the jaw opens and shuts and the legs move.

The bird's wings move up and down.

Make a sketch of your model and then cut the pieces out of cardboard. Pierce holes through the parts where the "joint" will be and push a split pin through the holes. Flatten out the ends of the pin, so that it doesn't fall out. It is easier to paint the pieces of your model before you fit the pins.

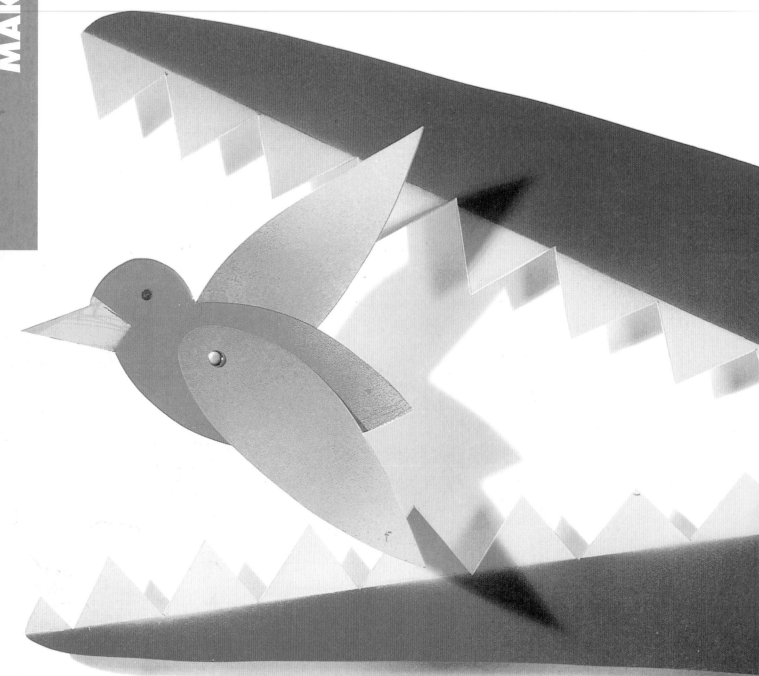

By making simple slits in pieces of cardboard, you will be able to make almost any cardboard shape stand up on its own!

Make slits a little wider than a single cut, so that the pieces slot together neatly. On one cardboard shape, the slit should start at the top. On the other cardboard shape, it should start at the bottom. Slits should usually be slightly more than half the height of the shape. The picture on this page show different methods for slitting and slotting cardboard shapes together.

You can also make a flat piece of cardboard stand up by folding it down the middle.

These pop-up cards are made by cutting and scoring. The main shapes stay attached to the card by tabs. First, mark the center of a piece of cardboard. Draw the main part of your picture on the lower half of the card. Decide which parts of the picture you want joined up. Draw in the tabs. You will need two if it is a big drawing. The length of the tabs should be equal to the distance from the bottom of your drawing to the center fold. Look at the picture opposite. The blue lines show score lines. Cut and score your picture and tabs, and push them out from the background.

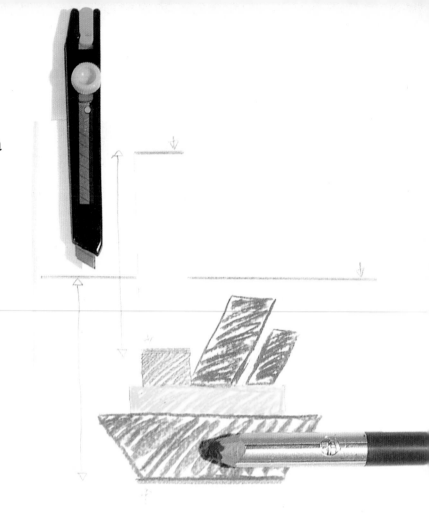

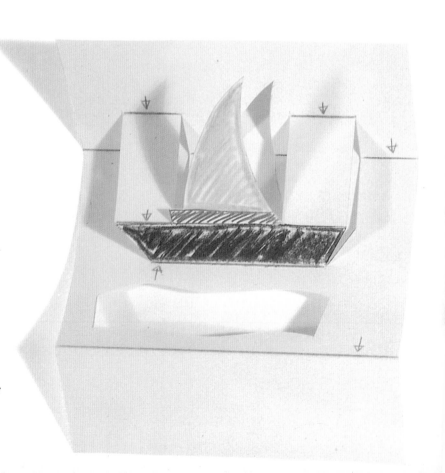

To make your card move, fold under one edge of the card and tape it down to make a pocket. Cut a strip of cardboard slightly longer than the pocket. Pull the strip in and out!

Create your own theater, actors, and scenery from a shoe box and some pieces of cardboard! Invite your friends and act out your favorite plays with your own characters. On the next two pages, you will find out how we made our theater by slotting in some scenery from the top and moving other pieces backward and forward from the sides.

Use a shoe box or a fruit box to make the frame for your theater. Cut a hole at one of the narrow ends, leaving a narrow frame. Make a decorated front from a piece of thin cardboard and glue it to the frame.

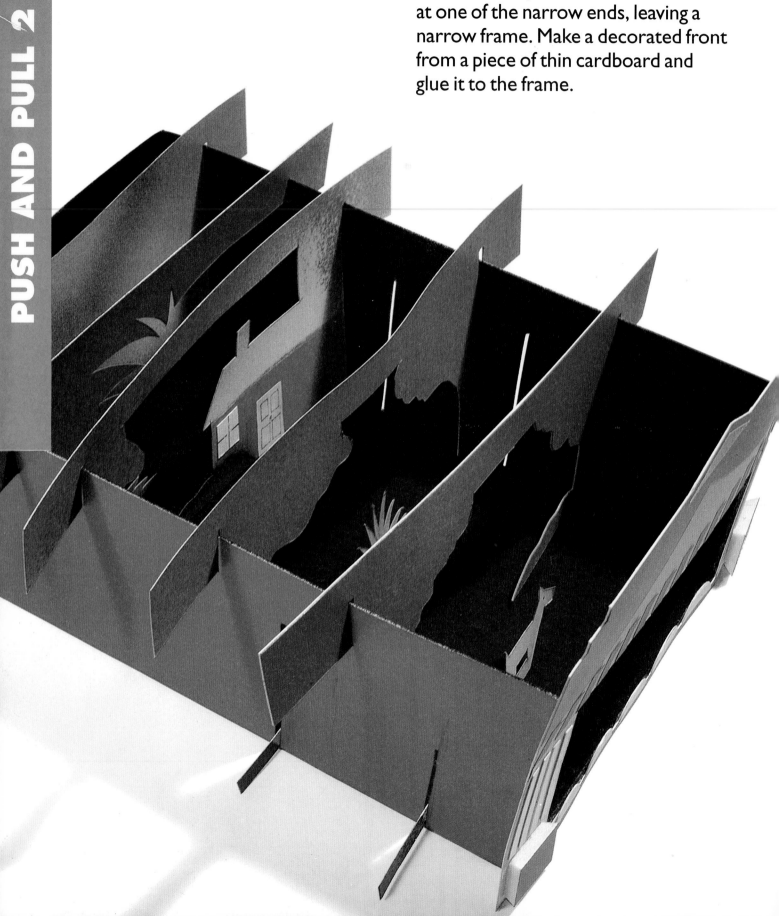

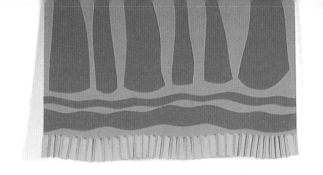

Make a selection of backdrops from pieces of thin cardboard. The backdrops should be slightly higher than the shoe box. Cut slits – about as wide as three knife cuts – so that the backdrops slot comfortably over the box. The distance from the top of the slot to the bottom of the backdrop should be the same height as the box. You can make curtains for your theater in the same way.

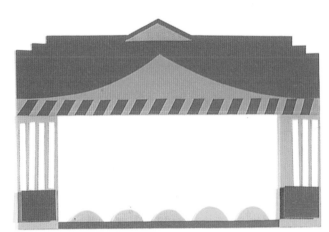

To make characters and props, draw and cut out the shapes, leaving a length of thin cardboard attached. Make slits along the side of the box, high enough to push the characters and props through.

Here are some delicious fruit and vegetables – but they are not for eating! They are all made from papier mâché – a mixture of paste and paper. On the next page, you will find the paste recipe and tips for making the basic framework.

Paste Recipe

1. Measure out a cup of flour and 3 cups of water.

2. In a pan, mix a little of the water with the flour to make a smooth paste.

3. Add the rest of the water and ask a grown-up to heat the mixture until it boils – stirring all the time! Turn the heat down and let the mixture simmer until the paste thickens.

4. Leave the mixture until it is cold.

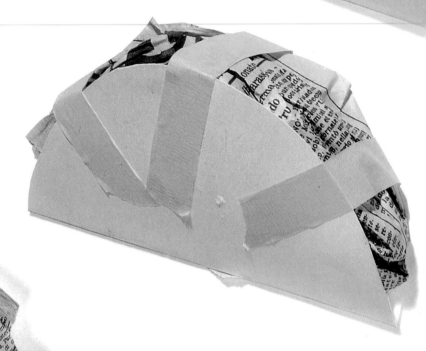

Decide what shape you want your finished object to be. Make a framework from cardboard and newspaper, using Scotch™ tape to keep it in position. Paste on layers of newspaper, molding the layers as you go along to make a good shape. Leave your object to dry. Then paint and varnish it.

MODELS

CONTENTS

All the things on these pages have been used somewhere in the MODELS section of this book. You should be able to find them all at home or at school.

Some modeling material is very sticky and hard to get off certain surfaces, so you should always cover the space you are working on. Make sure you ask a grown-up before using things from around the home.

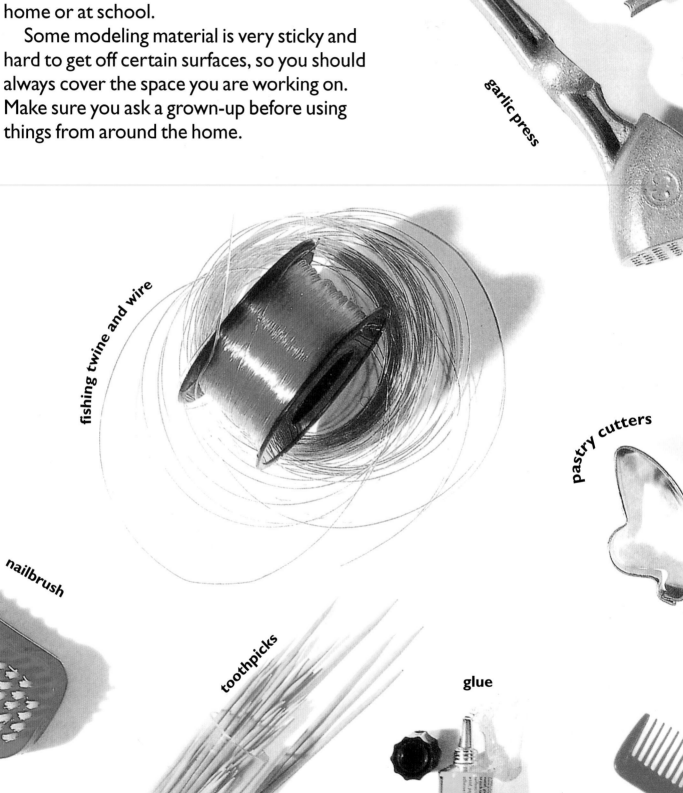

garlic press

fishing twine and wire

pastry cutters

nailbrush

toothpicks

glue

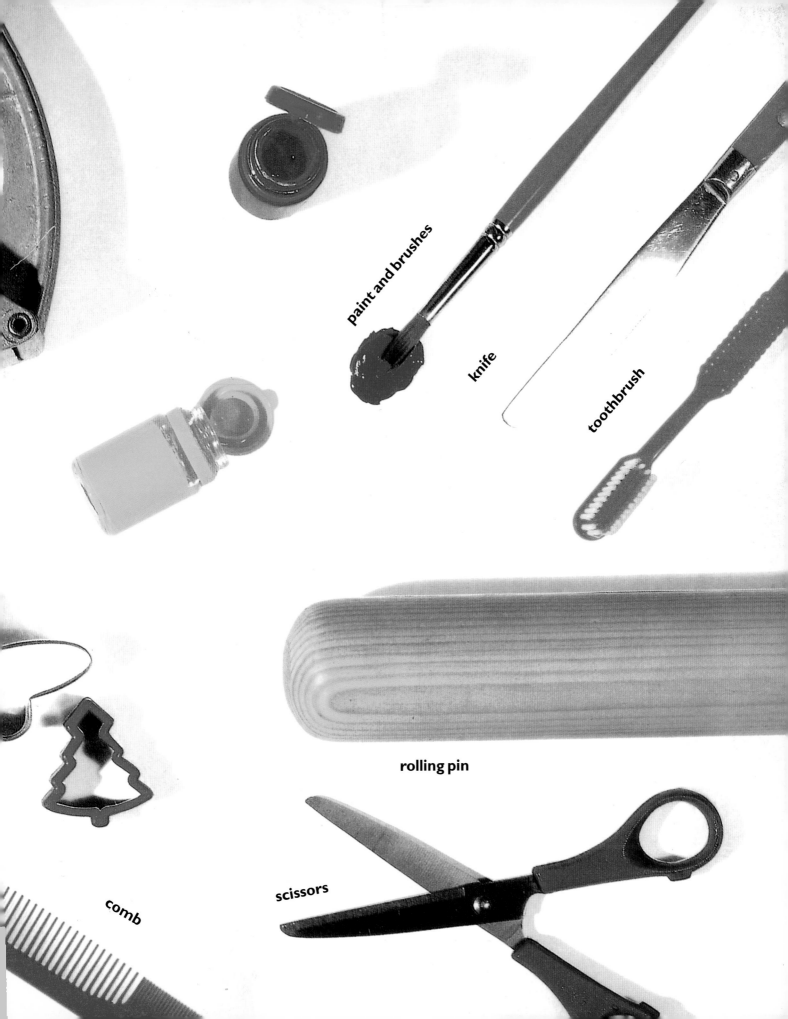

paint and brushes

knife

toothbrush

rolling pin

comb

scissors

Modeling dough is very easy to make and you can use it again and again. The recipe is on page 116. Press it and roll it into shape and use different colors. Decorate your models with other things, such as the fishing twine and sequins that make up these fireworks. Modeling dough is good for molding too because it takes on the shape of the container it is put in.

Modeling Dough Recipe
2¹/₂ cups flour   ¹/₂ cup salt
1 cup water   2 tablespoons oil
4 tablespoons cream of tartar
food coloring

1. Mix together all the ingredients in a bowl except the food coloring. Put the mixture in a pan and stir in enough coloring to get the color you want.

2. Ask a grown-up to stir the mixture over a low heat until it forms into a ball.

You can use your modeling dough again
and again as long as you store it in a
sealed container or a plastic bag.

You can make permanent decorations, such as Christmas ornaments or mobiles, with salt dough.

Salt Dough Recipe

1 $^3/_4$ cups plain flour
1 cup salt
1 tablespoon wallpaper paste powder
1 cup and 2 tablespoons water

1. Mix together the dry ingredients, then add the water. Roll out the dough out to a $^1/_4$-inch thickness. Cut out shapes. With a toothpick, make holes in the shapes to push ribbons through when they have been baked.
2. Lay wax paper on a cookie sheet. Place the shapes on the paper and bake for 8 hours in a warm oven (225°F).
3. When they have cooled, the models can be painted with poster paints. Allow the paint to dry before adding two coats of varnish. This seals the dough and stops the decorations from getting moldy.

Non-hardening modeling clay can be used over and over again. There are lots of ways to use it – you can join pieces just by pressing them together. Give the clay a marbled effect by rolling two or three different colors into a ball. Use things such as a nailbrush or a garlic press to make many different shapes and textures.

Making pottery is easier than you imagine! Clay is inexpensive and available in most craft stores. If you make mistakes, you can always start again.

Try making a "pinch" pot by pressing your thumb into a ball of clay and gradually hollowing it out. Or make a "coil" pot by building up long "sausages" of clay.

To stop the clay from drying out, keep it sealed in plastic or wrapped in a damp cloth.

Make some "slip" from leftover fragments of clay soaked in water. You use the slip to keep the clay you are working with moist and to help stick pieces together. Use an old toothbrush to apply the slip.

Roll out your clay on a smooth surface and cut out shapes using a knife or cookie cutters.

Make a "slab" pot by cutting out squares of clay and sticking them to a base. Rub over the joints with plenty of slip until they are smooth. You can smooth out your coil pot with slip too.

Clay has to be baked in a kiln to make it hard and strong. If you don't have a kiln at school, ask at a library or craft store where you can find one.

Decorate your pottery while it is still wet by pressing on shapes or making patterns in the clay. When it has been baked, you can paint or varnish it.